Cottonmouths

by Colleen Sexton

BELLWETHER MEDIA · MINNEAPOLIS, MN

Note to Librarians, Teachers, and Parents:

Blastoff! Readers are carefully developed by literacy experts and combine standards-based content with developmentally appropriate text.

Level 1 provides the most support through repetition of high-frequency words, light text, predictable sentence patterns, and strong visual support.

Level 2 offers early readers a bit more challenge through varied simple sentences, increased text load, and less repetition of high-frequency words.

Level 3 advances early-fluent readers toward fluency through increased text and concept load, less reliance on visuals, longer sentences, and more literary language.

Level 4 builds reading stamina by providing more text per page, increased use of punctuation, greater variation in sentence patterns, and increasingly challenging vocabulary.

Level 5 encourages children to move from "learning to read" to "reading to learn" by providing even more text, varied writing styles, and less familiar topics.

Whichever book is right for your reader, Blastoff! Readers are the perfect books to build confidence and encourage a love of reading that will last a lifetime!

This edition first published in 2011 by Bellwether Media, Inc.

No part of this publication may be reproduced in whole or in part without written permission of the publisher. For information regarding permission, write to Bellwether Media, Inc., Attention: Permissions Department, 5357 Penn Avenue South, Minneapolis, MN 55419.

Library of Congress Cataloging-in-Publication Data

Sexton, Colleen A., 1967-
  Cottonmouths / by Colleen Sexton.
    p. cm. – (Blastoff! readers: Snakes alive)
  Includes bibliographical references and index.
  Summary: "Simple text and full-color photography introduce beginning readers to cottonmouths. Developed by literacy experts for students in kindergarten through third grade"–Provided by publisher.
  ISBN 978-1-60014-454-7 (hardcover : alk. paper)
  1. Agkistrodon piscivorus–Juvenile literature. I. Title.
  QL666.O69S485 2010
  597.96'3–dc22   2010000709

Text copyright © 2011 by Bellwether Media, Inc.
Printed in the United States of America, North Mankato, MN.

080110   1162

Contents

Cottonmouths are large, **poisonous** snakes. They are named for the color inside of their mouths. It is white like cotton.

Cottonmouths have flat, triangle-shaped heads and narrow necks. Tough **scales** cover their thick bodies.

Most cottonmouths grow to be 3 to 5 feet (1 to 1.5 meters) long.

Cottonmouths can be green, black, or tan. They have brown stripes and spots. Their bellies are pale yellow or cream-colored.

Young cottonmouths have colorful bodies and yellow tails. Their skin gets darker as they grow older.

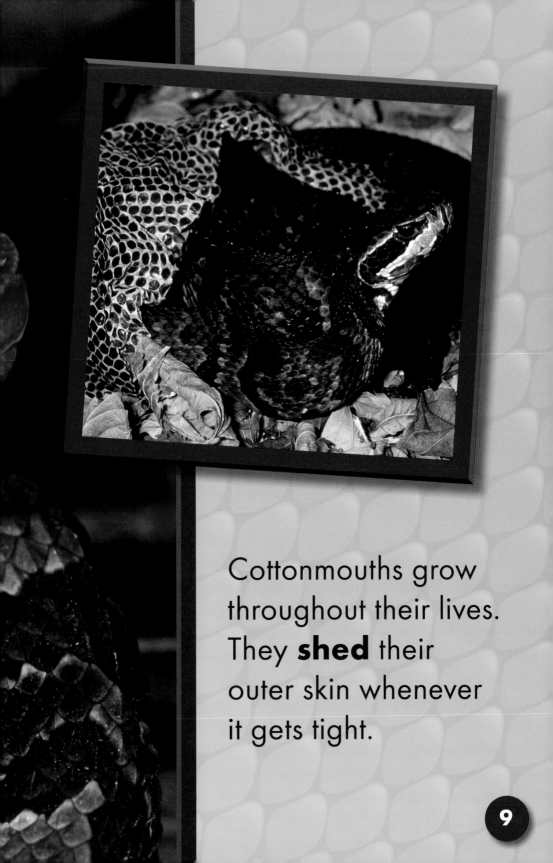

Cottonmouths grow
throughout their lives.
They **shed** their
outer skin whenever
it gets tight.

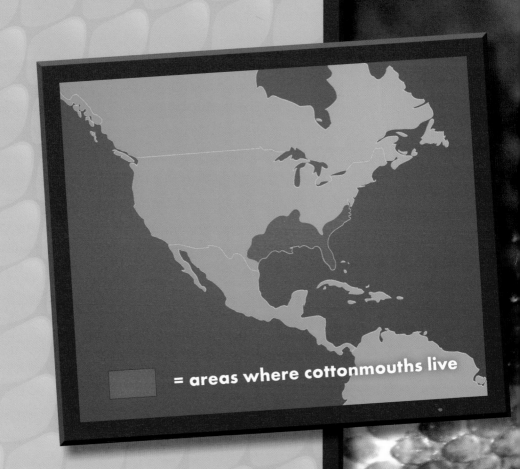

= areas where cottonmouths live

Cottonmouths live
in the southeastern
United States.
They live near
swamps, rivers,
and lakes.

Cottonmouths hunt **prey** both on land and in the water.

heat-sensing pits

Cottonmouths have two **pits** on their heads that sense the body heat of prey. They use forked tongues to smell the air.

Cottonmouths wait for prey to come near. They eat animals such as fish, birds, frogs, and mice.

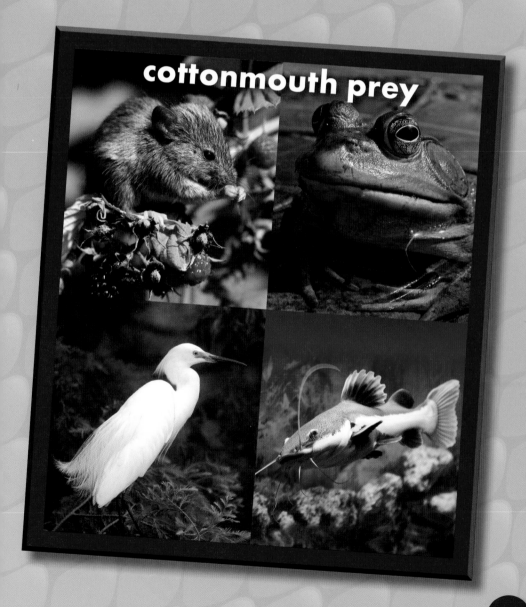

cottonmouth prey

Sometimes they wait for prey in **shallow** water. They poke their heads above water as they swim.

Sometimes cottonmouths wait for prey in branches above water. They slide into the water when they sense prey is near.

Cottonmouths bite their prey with sharp, curved **fangs**. A poison called **venom** flows through the fangs and into the bite.

The venom makes the prey stop breathing and die. A cottonmouth often holds its prey underwater until the animal stops moving.

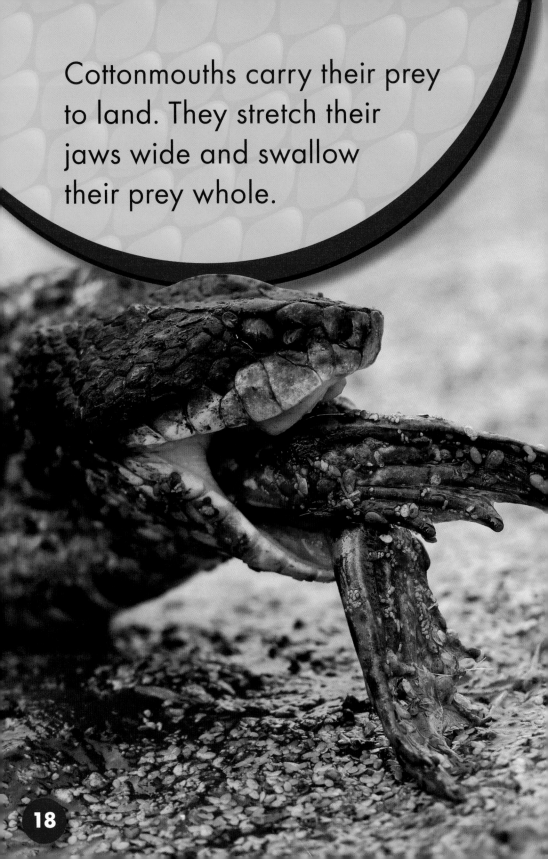

Cottonmouths carry their prey to land. They stretch their jaws wide and swallow their prey whole.

alligator

Cottonmouths can be prey too. They hide from alligators, snapping turtles, eagles, and other **predators**.

Sometimes a cottonmouth comes face-to-face with a predator. It **coils** its body and moves its tail back and forth as a warning.

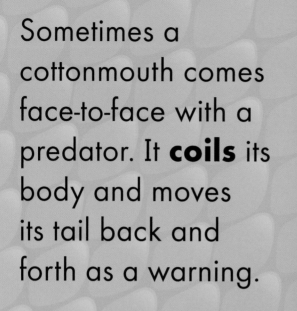

The cottonmouth is ready to **gape**. It throws back its head. It opens its white mouth wide and scares away the predator!

Glossary

coils—winds into loops

fangs—sharp, curved teeth; cottonmouths have hollow fangs through which venom can move into a bite.

gape—to stare at something with a wide-open mouth; cottonmouths are the only snakes that gape.

pits—areas of a snake's face that sense the body heat of an animal; pits tell a snake where an animal is and how big it is.

poisonous—able to kill or harm with a poison; the venom that a cottonmouth makes is a poison.

predators—animals that hunt other animals for food

prey—animals that are hunted by other animals for food

scales—small plates of skin that cover and protect a snake's body

shallow—not deep

shed—to let something fall off; snakes rub their bodies against rocks or trees to help shed their skin.

swamps—wet, spongy areas of land that are often covered with water

venom—a poison that some snakes make; cottonmouth venom is deadly.

To Learn More

AT THE LIBRARY

Feldman, Heather. *Cottonmouths*. New York, N.Y.: PowerKids Press, 2004.

Gibbons, Gail. *Snakes*. New York, N.Y.: Holiday House, 2007.

Gunzi, Christiane. *The Best Book of Snakes*. New York, N.Y.: Kingfisher, 2003.

ON THE WEB

Learning more about cottonmouths is as easy as 1, 2, 3.

1. Go to www.factsurfer.com.

2. Enter "cottonmouths" into the search box.

3. Click the "Surf" button and you will see a list of related Web sites.

With factsurfer.com, finding more information is just a click away.

Index